PROJECTS

T0308540

WELCOME TO
Country House

The smell of natural wood
could always create
the atmosphere of coziness and warmth.

LITTLE TOWN COASTERS

Finished coaster: *6″ × 6″*

Whenever someone visits my home, the first thing I do is to pull out my handmade coasters and serve coffee or tea on them. It always makes my guests smile and feel that they are specially treated. These little house coasters are a quick project that will sweetly dress up your teatime.

Materials and Supplies

Dimensions are written width × height throughout.

Linen: 7″ × 7″ for coaster front

Backing: 6½″ × 6½″ for coaster back

Fabric scraps for houses

Cotton batting: 7″ × 7″

Thread: Neutral (ivory) and beige and gray embroidery floss

Cutting

For the house motifs, see the Little Town Coasters patterns (pullout page P1).

Fabric scraps: 4 squares 2″ × 2″

Minki Kim

ZAKKA

from the heart

Sew 16 Charming Projects
to Warm Any Home

stashBOOKS

an imprint of C&T Publishing

Publisher: Amy Marson

Creative Director: Gailen Runge

Acquisitions Editor: Roxane Cerda

Managing Editor: Liz Aneloski

Editor: Karla Menaugh

Technical Editor: Debbie Rodgers

Cover/Book Designer: April Mostek

Font Designer: Minki Kim

Production Coordinator: Tim Manibusan

Production Editor: Jennifer Warren

Illustrator: Linda Johnson

Photo Assistant: Rachel Holmes

Cover photography by Minki Kim; **interior photography** by Minki Kim, unless otherwise noted

Published by Stash Books, an imprint of C&T Publishing, Inc., P.O. Box 1456, Lafayette, CA 94549

Library of Congress Cataloging-in-Publication Data

Names: Kim, Minki, 1973- author.

Title: Zakka from the heart : sew 16 charming projects to warm any home / Minki Kim.

Description: Lafayette, CA : Stash Books, an imprint of C&T Publishing, Inc., 2019.

Identifiers: LCCN 2018061273 | ISBN 9781617458514 (soft cover)

Subjects: LCSH: Sewing. | House furnishings. | Notions (Merchandise)

Classification: LCC TT715 .K5555 2019 | DDC 646.4--dc23

LC record available at https://lccn.loc.gov/2018061273

Printed in China

10 9 8 7 6 5 4 3 2 1

Dedication

For Dad and Mom and my sister and brother in Korea.

I miss you each day.

Acknowledgments

I am very grateful to the following:

Roxane Cerda and Amy Marson, who always listen to my ideas and support me from the beginning to the end, and Karla Menaugh, for her help and for making the book easy to read.

All my Riley Blake Designs family, Alex Veronelli and Erin Sampson from Aurifil threads, Lindsey Grand from The Warm Company, Sara SJ Kim from Dailylike Canada, Annie Unrein from ByAnnie, Yvonne Busdeker from OLFA Craft North America, Raymond Choi from Byhands Hand Craft USA, LECIEN, Alice Voss-Kantor from BERNINA USA, and Leslie Routson from Taylored Expressions. I truly appreciate you trusting me and supporting me without question.

My little Claire, who always plays around me, keeps me company, and loves everything Mom makes. And my Chloe and Caylin, who always share the most honest feedback that helps me to try another and another.

My husband, Alex, for being my best pal.

contents

Introduction   6

Projects   9

introduction

I remember the very first handmade item gifted to me from my mom and dad: a gray indoor shoe bag for my first day of first grade. When I was a child in Korea, my classmates and I had to change from outdoor shoes to indoor shoes before entering the classroom. Everybody wore the same white cloth indoor shoes, and every Monday our teacher checked to see if we had washed them during the weekend. Most kids brought a store-bought shoe bag with colorful cartoon characters, but mine was my parents' collaboration. My dad sewed the bag with handles and my mom hand appliquéd a bunny from an old blanket to decorate the plain bag. I used it until I wore a hole in it. (Eventually I lost a pair of shoes through that hole!) Whenever I think of my shoe bag, I realize how much my parents loved me and how a young married couple tried to give a special gift to their first child. It took me 30 years to come to that realization.

Time has passed, and I have three children, just like my parents. Now I see myself in my daughter. She changes her lunch bag whenever I make a new one. Her best friend expects to receive something handmade on her birthday. Sometimes she even hints to my daughter about what she wants: "I want the same pencil case you have." I think making things by hand is a very healthy habit that nurtures our busy lives. And I have found that giving handmade gifts is addictive in a very good way.

In this book, I have tried to include projects that are both inspirational and informational. I have included as many step-by-step photos as possible for beginners. For advanced sewists, I tried to introduce a variety of projects and details that you can adapt to your own style.

It is my hope that you will flip through this book whenever you are searching for a project idea, a quick handmade gift, or just some simple hand sewing to calm your busy mind. Many projects are simple and can be finished in an afternoon, yet each of them has unique details. I believe that attention to one little detail makes all the difference.

I hope you turn the pages over and over, twist a bit of a design, or mix and match for another new project, like an appliquéd strawberry drawstring bag or embroidered zipper pouch. The imagination is endless, and I hope we can stitch what we see in our everyday lives uniquely and kindly together.

minki

Downloadable Patterns

All the full-size patterns for the projects are located on the pullout. You can also download and print any of the patterns at **tinyurl.com/11356-patterns-download**. Make sure you print the images at 100%!

Instructions

Seam allowances are ¼˝ unless otherwise noted.

REVERSE APPLIQUÉ THE HOUSES

1. Using a pencil or temporary marking pen, trace the houses onto the linen square, 1½˝ from the bottom and 1¼˝ from the right side.

2. With a pair of scissors, clip the center of each house and cut out the linen, leaving a ¼˝ seam allowance inside the house. Clip into each corner for easy folding. Fold the seams inside and press. ┊ A & B

3. Sew 2 fabric scraps together. If you want to use the print on the fabric as a window or door, mark the roof's sewing line on the house fabric before adding the roof fabric. Lay each house on a piece of batting. ┊ C

4. Place the linen square from Step 2 on top of the scraps on the batting. Make sure the roof is in the right place. Press. ┊ D

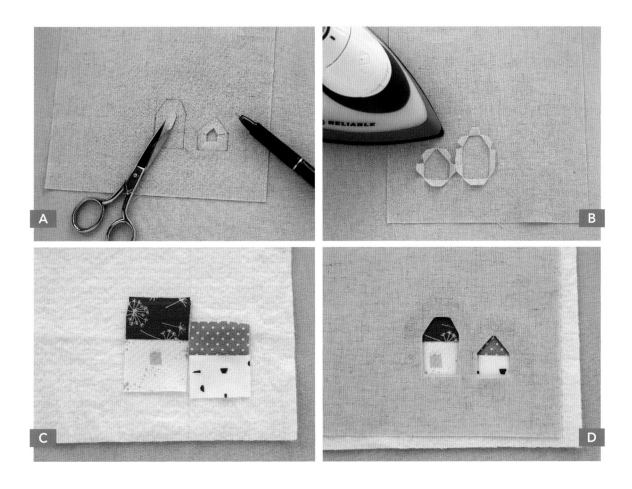

5. Pin the linen to the batting and place a running stitch around the houses, using 2 strands of gray embroidery floss. Stitch right through the linen and batting. Trim to 6½″ × 6½″. ¦ E

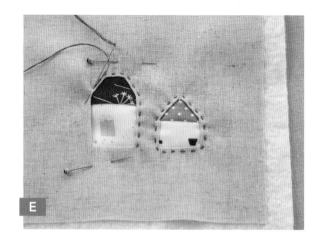

tip

You can also machine stitch around the houses using dark thread. Draw additional designs as you desire. I added a television antenna to one house and a little window to the other.

ASSEMBLE THE COASTERS

1. Place the coaster front and back right sides facing and stitch together, leaving a gap for turning. Turn. Hand stitch the gap closed.

2. Topstitch around the edge of the coaster by hand (using 2 strands of embroidery floss) or by machine.

tip

When topstitching by hand, pull the thread just a little. This creates nice wrinkles that add a handmade charm.

MACARON PINCUSHION

Finished pincushion: 3˝ diameter × 2½˝ high

The best reward of giving is when you see that your gifts are frequently used and loved. Pincushions are good pals for sewing friends. Peeking at my pincushion on my friend's sewing table makes me smile. I hope you give a box of hand-stitched macarons and receive that happy moment in return.

Materials and Supplies

Dimensions are written width × height throughout.

Print: 8˝ × 8˝

Cotton batting: 8˝ × 8˝

Polyester fiberfill

Embroidery floss

Cutting

For the circles, see the Macaron Pincushion patterns (pullout page P2).

Print: 4 circles 3¼˝ diameter

Cotton batting: 4 circles 3˝ diameter

Instructions

MAKE THE MACARON

Seam allowances are ¼˝ unless otherwise noted.

1. Sew 2 print circles all the way around, right sides together. Clip the center of one circle and turn it right side out through the opening. ┊ A

2. Using a matching-color thread, make a running stitch ⅛˝ from the circle's edge. Pull the thread until the edge is nicely gathered, as shown. ┊ B

3. Tie a knot and pull the thread inside the center. Cut. Stuff the pincushion with polyester fiberfill until it resembles a macaron. Make sure it's not firm.

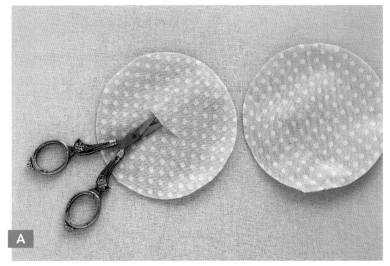

A

B

4. Repeat Steps 1–3 to make a pair of macarons. ┊ C

5. Stack 4 layers of cotton batting. Using scissors, cut a 3˝ circle from the stack. ┊ D

6. Pin the batting stack between the 2 macaron circles. With matching-color thread, start stitching ½˝ from the outer circle. Stitch the batting and macarons together through the layers. Trim the batting if necessary. ┊ E

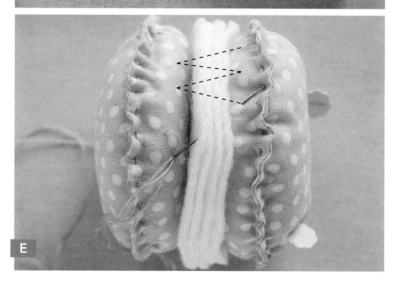

POCKET DRAWSTRING BAG

Finished bag: *6˝ wide × 9˝ high × 6˝ deep*

I have enjoyed making drawstring bags with all kinds of details. When I am in a hurry to leave home or to give someone a gift, however, a simple and light drawstring bag gets the pick. This bag is assembled in an unusual way and is a good use for your fabric scraps, as well! If you want a different-size bag, just enlarge or reduce the pattern as desired.

Materials and Supplies

Dimensions are written width × height throughout.

Assorted prints: 4 rectangles 6½˝ × 12½˝ for bag

Accent fabric: ⅛ yard

Lining: ⅜ yard *or* 6½˝ × 12½˝ scraps of 4 fabrics

¼˝-wide cord: 31˝ length

½˝-wide cotton ribbon: 1½˝ length

⅝˝ round wood bead (*optional*)

Cutting

For the bag panel and pocket patterns, see the Pocket Drawstring Bag patterns (pullout pages P1 and P2).

Assorted prints: 4 bag panels

Accent fabric

• 2 pockets

• 1 strip 26˝ × 2½˝ for the channel

Lining: 4 bag panels

Instructions

Seam allowances are ¼″ unless otherwise noted.

MAKE THE POCKET

Fold the cotton ribbon in half. Pin the 2 pockets right sides together and slip the ribbon into the seam on the right side, 1″ from the top raw edge. Line up the raw edges of the ribbon with the raw edges of the pockets; the ribbon fold will be inside the pocket pieces. Sew the 2 pockets together all the way around, leaving a 2″ gap for turning. Clip each corner seam to give a nice corner shape. Turn right side out and press. ┆ A

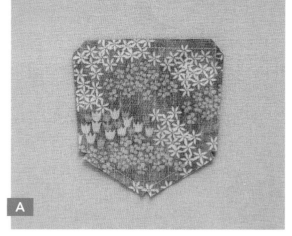

MAKE THE BAG EXTERIOR

1. Center the pocket on a bag panel, 3″ from the top raw edge. Topstitch around the sides and bottom of the pocket. Backstitch 2–3 times on both sides of the pocket opening for strength. ┆ B

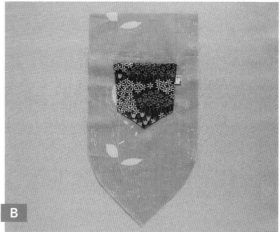

2. Sew 2 bag panels together along one long side, right sides together. Repeat with the other 2 panels. Sew the pairs together to finish the bag shape. ┆ C

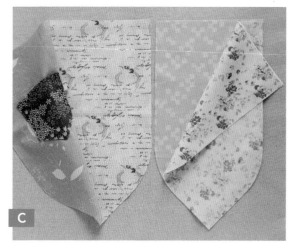

MAKE THE LINING

Sew the bag lining together following Make the Bag Exterior (above), except leave a 3″ gap in one seam for turning. ┆ D

ASSEMBLE THE BAG

1. Slide the lining inside the bag, right sides together. Match the seams. ┊ E

2. Fold each short end of the channel strip 1″ to the wrong side and press. Fold the strip in half lengthwise with wrong sides together and press.

3. Insert the channel between the lining and the exterior, aligning the top raw edges. Pin in place. ┊ F

tip

To make sure the cord insert goes to the side of the bag, lay the bag with the pocket centered, and place the channel ends on the side before you pin.

4. Stitch all the way around the top of the bag.

5. Tie a safety pin to the end of the cord or wrap a bit of tape on the cut ends of the cord to make it easy to insert through the channel. Starting with the opening on the right side of the bag, thread the cord all the way through the drawstring channel. Slide on a wooden bead before tying a knot to finish. ┊ G

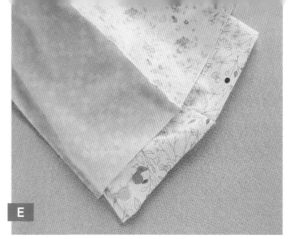

E

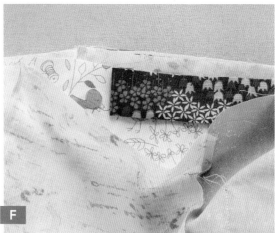

F

G

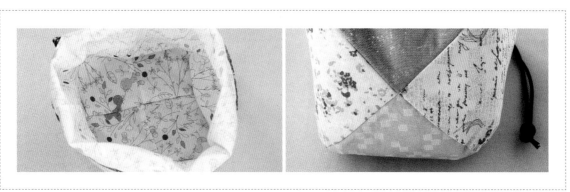

STITCHED COVER

Finished cover: 13½″ × 13½″

I have always dreamed about country living—raising chickens and planting all kinds of wildflowers that I could enjoy from the porch. This design was inspired by my beloved country living. A stitched cover is so useful for covering your basket, hanging in the kitchen as a dish towel, or as inspiring wall art! I hope you enjoy stitching and using your stitched cover.

Materials and Supplies

Dimensions are written width × height throughout.

Assorted wool felt scraps for appliqué pieces

Linen: Fat quarter for background

Backing: Fat quarter

> *tip*
>
> **When you are using two different types of fabrics, I think it is best to prewash them.**

Print scrap *or* **cotton ribbon** for tab

Cotton embroidery floss: I used COSMO brand in the following colors:

Yellow (300)	Orange (146)
Dark pink (2115)	Coffee (2307)
Light pink (833)	Teal (374)
Dark purple (477)	Light purple (814)

Cutting

Linen: 1 square 14″ × 14″

Backing: 1 square 14″ × 14″

Print scrap *or* **cotton ribbon:** 1 rectangle 2½″ × 2″ or a 2½″ length of ½″-wide ribbon

Instructions

Seam allowances are ¼″ unless otherwise noted.

For the embroidery design, see the Stitched Cover pattern (pullout page P2). See Embroidery Stitches (page 111) for instructions on how to make the stitches. Use 3 strands of embroidery floss for all hand embroidery.

STITCH THE EMBROIDERY DESIGN

1. Center and trace the embroidery design on the linen square.

2. Stitch the embroidery design, following the diagram below.

ASSEMBLE THE COVER

1. Place the linen and backing squares right sides together. Near one corner, slip in the folded fabric tab or a folded ribbon for the tab. Line up the short raw edges of the folded scrap or ribbon with the raw edges of the squares; the folded end will be inside the squares as you stitch.

Sew around the outer edge, leaving a 3″ gap for turning.

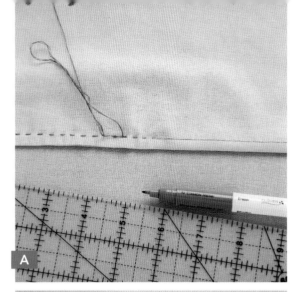

tip

It's easiest to use a ribbon for the tab. But if you are like me and don't have ribbon on hand when you want to make the cover, fold the print scrap in half lengthwise, wrong sides together, so it measures 1″ × 2½″. Open the scrap and fold the long edges to the inside fold. Refold so the scrap measures ½″ × 2½″. Topstitch along both folded edges to finish the tab.

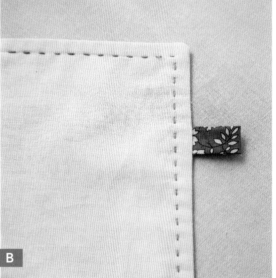

2. Turn right side out and hand stitch the gap closed. Press.

3. Use a temporary fabric pen to draw a line ½″ from the edge all the way around. Using 2 strands of light-purple embroidery floss, make a running stitch on the line. To end, tie a knot and hide it between the layers. ┊ A & B

tip

To hide a knot, put the needle right under the knot and push it about 1″ away. Pull the thread through and cut the thread.

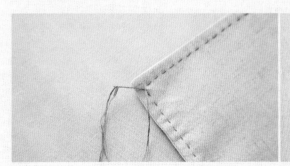

ROLL CAKE PENCIL CASE

Finished case: 3˝ diameter × 8˝ long

Sewing curved seams can be tricky if you are not used to it. This round case needs neither curved-seam experience nor binding. Assemble the sides by hand to finish this cute pencil case quickly and easily.

Materials and Supplies

Dimensions are written width × height throughout.

Print 1: Fat eighth *or* 8½˝ × 10½˝ scrap for case body

Print 2: 8˝ × 4˝ for case sides

Lining: Fat quarter

Fabric scrap: 3˝ × 3˝ for zipper tabs

Medium-weight fusible fleece: Fat quarter

Hand-quilting thread

8˝ zipper

Optional patch supplies:

  Linen: 3˝ × 2¼˝

  Felt scraps

  Fusible interfacing: 3˝ × 2¼˝

  Embroidery floss

Cutting

For the pencil case and flower patterns, see the Roll Cake Pencil Case patterns (pullout page P2).

Print 1: 1 rectangle 8½˝ × 10½˝

Print 2: 2 case sides

Lining

• 1 rectangle 8½˝ × 10½˝ for the body lining

• 2 case sides for the side lining

Fabric scrap: 2 rectangles 1½˝ × 3˝

Medium-weight fusible fleece

• 1 rectangle 8˝ × 10˝

• 2 case sides, trimmed on the inner line

• 2 tabs

Felt scraps (*optional*): 1 flower and 2 leaves

Instructions

Seam allowances are ¼˝ unless otherwise noted.

MAKE THE BODY

Center and fuse the 8˝ × 10˝ fleece on the wrong side of the case body. Place the case body and lining right sides together and stitch all the way around, leaving a 3˝ gap for turning. Turn right side out and hand stitch the gap closed. Press in shape. ┆ A

MAKE THE PATCH (*OPTIONAL*)

See Embroidery Stitches (page 111) for instructions on how to make the stitches.

1. Arrange the felt flower and leaves on the 3˝ × 2¼˝ linen rectangle. Hand stitch using 3 strands of embroidery floss. Use the whip-stitch for the flower and leaves and a chain stitch (page 111) for the stem. ┆ B

2. Use French knot stitches and 3 strands of embroidery floss for the flower stamen. (I wrap the needle twice for the French knot stitch.) ┆ C

3. Place the 3˝ × 2¼˝ fusible interfacing rectangle on top of the flower appliqué piece, with the fusible side facing the appliqué. Sew around the outer edge. Make a 1˝ clip in the center of the fusible interfacing and turn right side out.

4. Center the patch 1˝ below the top of the case, aligning the short edge, and press to fuse the interfacing to the case. Topstitch around the edge of the patch by machine. *Optional:* Use gray embroidery floss and a running stitch to hand stitch the patch to the case. ┆ D

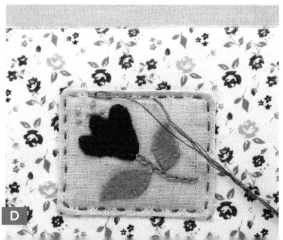

ADD THE ZIPPER

Place the zipper under the short edge of the case body, aligning the edge right next to the zipper teeth. Topstitch ⅛″ from the edge. Bring the opposite side of the case around and stitch it to the other side of the zipper in the same manner. Make sure to backstitch at the beginning and end of the zipper for strength. ¦ E & F

tip

If you use a lace zipper, place the zipper on top of the case body and topstitch it in place.

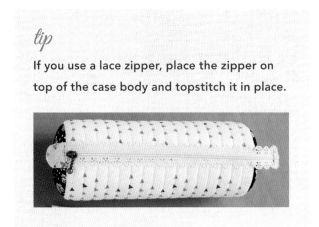

ADD THE ZIPPER TAB

1. Fold the 3″ scrap square in half, right sides together. Press ¼″ of the long raw edges to the wrong side of the fabric.

2. On one side of the folded square, tuck the fleece tab pieces into the ¼″ fold, with the straight edges aligned and about ½″ apart. Fuse the fleece tabs to the fabric; then stitch around the half-circle, just next to the fleece. Trim the seam allowance on each tab. Turn right side out and press to make 2 tabs. ¦ G

3. Slide the zipper ends into the tabs, trimming the raw edge of the zipper if necessary. Topstitch the tabs through all layers. Make sure to backstitch at the beginning and end of the zipper for strength. ¦ H

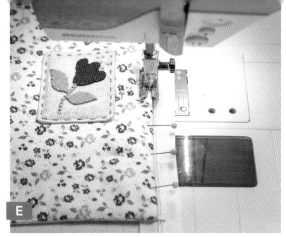

E

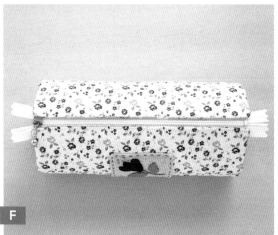

F

G

H

Roll Cake Pencil Case   31

MAKE THE SIDES

Center and fuse the fleece side circles on the wrong side of the case sides. Place a side circle and lining circle right sides together; stitch around the outer edge, leaving a 2″ gap for turning. Turn right side out and press. Hand stitch the gap closed. Make 2. | I

ASSEMBLE THE CASE

1. With the zipper closed, pin a side to the body. Hand stitch to attach the 2 pieces together. Use polyester hand-quilting thread for strength, and place your stitches in the outer fabrics for a clean finish. Stitch 3–4 small stitches at a time and pull the thread until the 2 pieces are attached with no gap.

2. Turn the case inside out and sew the side again, this time stitching through the inner fabrics. | J & K

> *tip*
>
> **Place the closed turning gap in the side under the zipper. That helps perfect the round case side.**

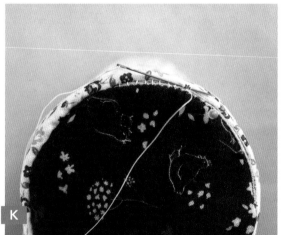

3. Repeat Steps 1 and 2 (above) to attach the other side to the case. | L

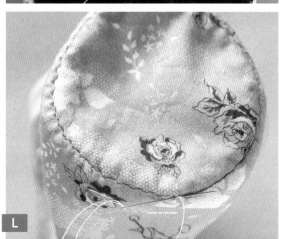

DATE NIGHT CLUTCH

Finished closed clutch: 11½″ × 7¾″

A clutch is a simple and beginner-friendly project. With an invisible magnet closure and heavyweight interfacing, you can make a wearable, stylish handbag. As a bonus, I'll show you how to make a tassel using fabric scraps that you can coordinate with any bag or purse!

Materials and Supplies

Dimensions are written width × height throughout.

Print: ½ yard (1 yard if directional) for exterior

Lining: ½ yard

20″-wide woven fusible interfacing: 1 yard (I used Pellon SF101 Shape-Flex.)

20″-wide medium-weight fusible interfacing: 1 yard (You can use 2 layers of Pellon 809 Décor-Bond if you don't have medium-weight fusible interfacing.)

Fusible web: ⅛ yard (I used Heat*n*Bond. You could also use fabric glue.)

Batting: ½ yard

Heavyweight thread: 4″ length or longer for tassel (I used a thread that's a lot like hemp cord.)

½″ sew-in magnetic snap set (available from byannie.com or craft stores)

1″ swivel snap hook (I got mine from byannie.com.)

Leather label: 1½″ × ¼″ (*optional*)

Cutting

See the Date Night Clutch pattern (pullout page P1).

Print

• 1 clutch body (If your fabric is directional, cut the length along the lengthwise grain of fabric.)

• 1 rectangle 4½″ × 7″ for the tassel

• 1 strip 1½″ × 2″ for the clutch tab

Lining: 1 rectangle 13″ × 21″

20″-wide woven fusible interfacing: 1 clutch body

20″-wide medium-weight fusible interfacing: 1 clutch body, trimmed on the inner line

Fusible web

• 1 strip 2″ × 7″ for the tassel

• 1 strip ½″ × 7″ for the tassel

• 1 strip ¾″ × 2″ for the clutch tab

Batting: 1 rectangle 13″ × 21″

Instructions

Seam allowances are ¼″ unless otherwise noted.

PREPARE THE EXTERIOR FABRIC

Fuse the woven interfacing to the wrong side of the exterior rectangle. Fuse the medium-weight interfacing to the woven interfacing. Protect your ironing board with a sheet of baking or parchment paper.

PREPARE THE LINING

Place the batting under the lining and pin or baste. Put a walking foot on your sewing machine and quilt as desired. (I drew a diagonal line as a guide using a Hera Marker, but you could also use a temporary marking pen. I then used matching thread and a 3.0 stitch length to sew diagonal lines 1″ apart.) Trim the batting to the outer line on the clutch pattern. ┊ A

ADD THE MAGNET BUTTON

Referring to the clutch pattern, mark the placement for the magnets on the wrong side of the lining. Attach one magnet with hand stitching to the flap and another to the lower edge. ┊ B & C

tip

Referring to the fold lines on the clutch pattern, fold the clutch and flap to be sure the magnets connect properly before you stitch them in place.

A

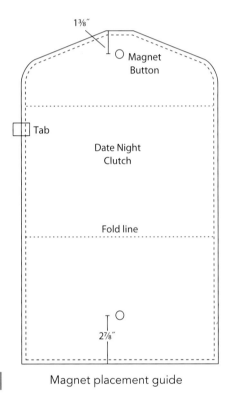

1⅜″

Magnet Button

Tab

Date Night Clutch

Fold line

2⅞″

B

Magnet placement guide

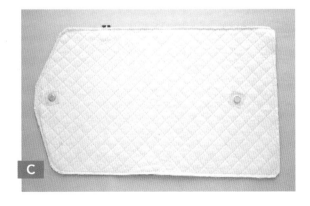

C

MAKE THE EXTERIOR

Pin or clip the exterior and lining with right sides together. Set aside. ┆ **D**

MAKE THE TAB

Center the ¾″ × 2″ fusible web rectangle on the wrong side of the 1½″ × 2″ exterior tab. Press to fuse in place. Peel off the paper and fold both raw edges of the exterior fabric toward the center. Press. Fold in half and slide between the exterior and lining, about 5½″ from the flap top. The short raw ends should line up with the raw edges of the clutch; the folded end will be inside. ┆ **E & F**

ASSEMBLE THE CLUTCH

1. Sew the exterior all the way around, leaving a gap for turning. Clip the curves and corners. Turn right side out through the gap and press in shape. Hand stitch the gap closed.

2. Fold up the bottom end of the clutch 7¼″ and double-check the magnetic closure; press in shape. Change to matching thread and topstitch both sides ⅛″ from the edge with a 3.0 stitch length. Backstitch at the beginning and end of each side for strength.

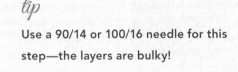

tip

Use a 90/14 or 100/16 needle for this step—the layers are bulky!

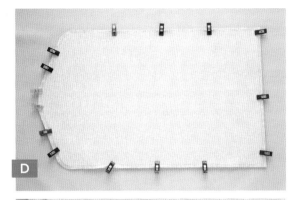

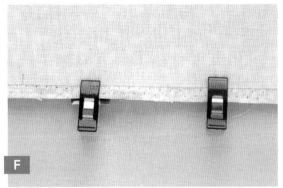

MAKE THE TASSEL

1. Press the 2″ × 7″ fusible web rectangle to the wrong side of the 4½″ × 7″ exterior fabric rectangle, ½″ from the top raw edge. ¦ G

2. Peel off the paper and fold the raw edges toward the center; press. ¦ H

3. Using a pair of scissors, cut parallel slits approximately ⅛″ apart, stopping ½″ from the top. ¦ I

4. Place the ½″ × 7″ fusible web strip on the uncut top section and press to fuse. ¦ J

5. Loop a heavyweight thread through the base of the swivel snap hook; then knot both ends together. Place the knot on the strip from Step 4 and roll the strip tight, pulling off the paper as you roll. Press well to secure. *Optional:* You can use permanent fabric glue instead of fusible web. ¦ K

6. Attach the tassel to the clutch through the tab. ¦ L

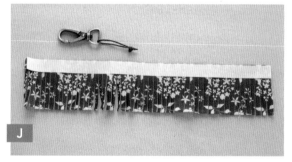

RUFFLE ZIPPER POUCH

Finished pouch: *6″ × 7″*

This cute zipper pouch makes the best handmade gift when a thankful moment comes. The ruffle pocket provides additional practical storage. If you are not confident with sewing the zipper in place along the curved edge, just change the zipper opening to a straight line. You will love it either way.

Materials and Supplies

Dimensions are written width × height throughout.

Print 1: 7″ × 8″ for pouch front

Print 2: 7″ × 6″ for pocket front

Print 3: Fat quarter for ruffle and pocket lining

Print 4: 7″ × 8″ for pouch back

Lining: Fat quarter

Woven fusible interfacing: ¼ yard
(I used Pellon SF101 Shape-Flex.)

Cotton batting: ¼ yard

8″ zipper (I recommend using a nylon zipper, which can be easily shortened if necessary.)

Cutting

For the pouch and pocket patterns, see the Ruffle Zipper Pouch patterns (pullout page P1).

Print 3

• 1 strip 2″ × 15″ for the ruffle

• 1 rectangle 7″ × 6″ for the pocket lining

Lining: 2 pouch bodies

Woven fusible interfacing

• 2 rectangles 7″ × 8″ for the body

• 1 rectangle 7″ × 6″ for the pocket

Cotton batting: 2 rectangles 7″ × 8″

Instructions

Seam allowances are ¼″ unless otherwise noted.

MAKE THE RUFFLED POCKET

1. Press the 2″ × 15″ ruffle strip in half lengthwise, wrong sides together. Change the setting on your sewing machine to loosen the tension to 0 and increase the stitch length to something like a basting stitch. Sew a straight line ⅛″ from the raw edges, tapering to the fold at each end. Pull the bottom thread to gather a ruffle that measures 1″ × 7″. Trim each end as shown. ┊ A & B

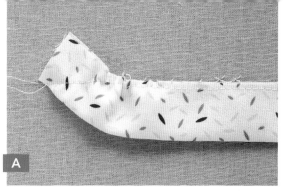

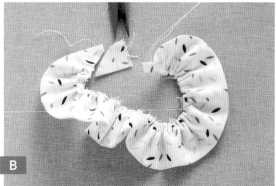

2. Fuse the 7″ × 6″ rectangle of woven fusible interfacing to the wrong side of the 7″ × 6″ pocket front. Trace the pocket pattern and trim the pocket to shape. Pin the ruffle to the pocket top, matching the raw edges. Sew the ruffle with a ¼″ seam allowance. ┊ C

3. Place the pocket lining and the ruffled pocket right sides together. Stitch along the top and clip the seam for nice and easy turning. ┊ D

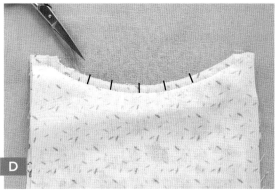

4. Fold the lining to the back and press in shape. Trim the excess lining even with the pocket front. ┊ E

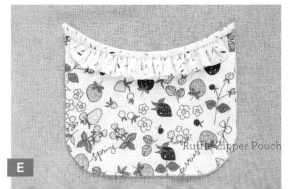

MAKE THE POUCH BODY

1. Fuse the 7″ × 8″ pieces of woven fusible interfacing to the wrong side of the pouch front and pouch back. Place the pouch pieces on top of the cotton batting; baste or press. Trace the pouch body pattern on both body pieces. Trim the excess. ┊ F

2. Place the pocket on top of the pouch body front, matching the bottom lines. Stitch with an ⅛″ seam allowance just to secure the pocket. ┊ G

Add the Zipper

Pin the zipper on top of the pouch front, matching the raw edges. Attach the zipper using a zipper foot. Pin the other side of the zipper to the pouch back and attach in the same manner. ┊ H

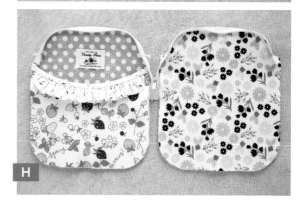

ASSEMBLE THE POUCH

1. Place the pouch front and pouch back right sides together. Leave the zipper open and sew all the way around. Trim the excess batting from the seam allowances to give a nice shape and turn right side out. ┊ I

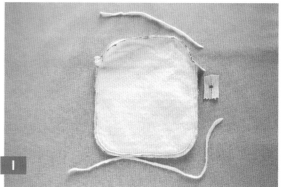

2. With right sides together, sew around the sides and bottom of the lining pieces. Use a ⅜″ seam allowance for a tight fit to the exterior. Put the lining inside the pouch, wrong sides together. Fold the top seam allowance of the lining to the wrong side and hand stitch the lining to the zipper to finish. ┊ J

TWO-IN-ONE ZIPPER POUCH

Finished pouch: *8″ × 7″*

A zipper pouch is always useful, but how cool would it be if it had another pocket? I got this idea when I saw my little girl digging in her purse, looking for her wee Littlest Pet Shop toys. It is great for sorting your notions or embroidery supplies and makes a great gift for someone special!

Materials and Supplies

Dimensions are written width × height throughout.

Print 1: Fat quarter for pouch exterior

Print 2: 8½″ × 2″ for pouch-exterior accent

Lining: Fat quarter

Midweight fusible interfacing: Fat quarter (I used Pellon 931TD Fusible Midweight.)

8″ zippers: 2

Cutting

Print 1

- 1 rectangle 8½″ × 7½″ for the pouch back
- 1 rectangle 8½″ × 5½″ for the outer pocket

Lining

- 2 rectangles 8½″ × 7½″ for the pouch
- 1 rectangle 8½″ × 6″ for the outer pocket
- 1 rectangle 8½″ × 5½″ for the outer pocket

Midweight fusible interfacing

- 1 rectangle 8″ × 7″
- 1 rectangle 8″ × 5″
- 1 rectangle 8″ × 1½″

Instructions

Seam allowances are ¼″ unless otherwise noted.

PREPARE THE EXTERIOR FABRIC

Center and fuse the interfacing pieces to the wrong side of the pouch back, outer pocket, and pouch exterior accent. Set aside.

ADD THE OUTER-POCKET ZIPPER

1. Lay the zipper on the outer pocket, right sides together. You will be able to see the wrong side of the zipper. Pin the zipper in place. Stitch together using a zipper foot, sewing ¼″ from the edge. Backstitch to secure. ┊ A

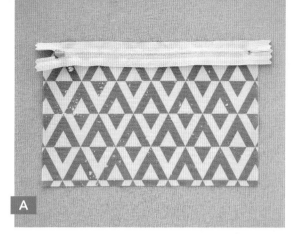

2. With right sides together, place the 8½″ × 5½″ outer-pocket lining piece on the back of the unit from Step 1, matching the top and side edges of the pouch exterior and the lining. Pin in place. Using a zipper foot, sew along the zipper through all layers. ┊ B

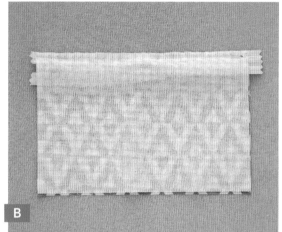

3. Reposition the fabrics wrong sides together and press. Topstitch ⅛″ from the pressed edge.

Place the 8½″ × 6″ outer-pocket lining piece under the other side of the zipper, right side up. Pin and sew ¼″ from the top edge with a zipper foot. ┊ C

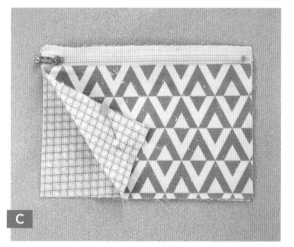

4. Align the pouch-exterior accent rectangle on the top edge of the zipper, wrong side up. Pin. Using a zipper foot, sew along the top edge. Press and topstitch. This unit should measure 8½″ × 7½″. ┊ D

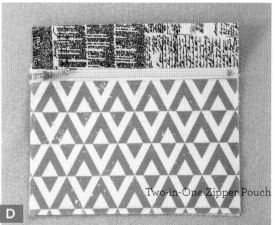

ADD THE POUCH ZIPPER

1. With right sides together, lay the zipper on the top of the print 2 rectangle. Make sure that both of the zipper pulls are positioned at the same side. Sew ¼″ from the edge. Press and topstitch. ┊ **E**

2. With right sides together, sew the pouch back to the other side of the zipper. Add the pouch lining piece to the back side of the zipper and stitch again. Press both pieces away from the zipper and topstitch. ┊ **F**

ASSEMBLE THE POUCH

1. Open the top zipper halfway. Position the pouch exterior pieces right sides together and the lining pieces right sides together. Push the seam allowance on either side of the zipper toward the lining.

2. Pin and sew along the bottom edge of the lining, leaving a gap at the bottom center. Sew along the remaining outer edge.

3. Turn right side out through the gap in the lining. Sew the gap closed by hand or machine. ┊ **G**

E

F

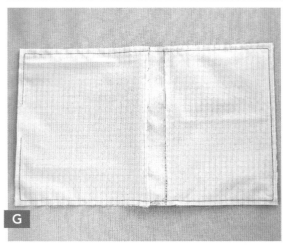

G

ON-THE-GO LIBRARY BAG

Finished bag: 10˝ wide × 8˝ high × 6˝ deep (+ 8˝-tall handles)

You will find so many uses for this bag with its open pocket on one side and a zipper pocket on the other! After trying many materials, I found that the right interfacing makes better bags and pouches. For my library bag, I used Décor-Bond (or you could use Deco-Fuse), which adds structure and defines form without cracking or adding weight. I also added a foam stabilizer to the lining for additional structure. To remove any wrinkles, steam press on a medium setting before starting. If you use a different batting, check the fit before you trim the batting.

Materials and Supplies

Dimensions are written width × height throughout.

Main print: ½ yard for bag exterior, lining, and binding

White print: ⅜ yard for pocket front and back

Accent print: Fat quarter for pocket

Bottom print: Fat quarter for bottom

Fusible interfacing: ½ yard (I prefer Pellon 809 Décor-Bond or Pellon 520 Deco-Fuse. I get my Décor-Bond from dailylike.ca.)

20˝-wide fusible webbing: 1 yard (I used Lite Steam-A-Seam 2.)

20˝-wide foam stabilizer: 1 yard (I like ByAnnie's Soft and Stable.)

Leather handles: 1 set ½˝ × 22˝ (I got mine from byhandsusa.com.)

7˝ zipper or longer (I recommend nylon teeth if you don't have the correct size.)

Cutting

For the bottom pattern, see the On-the-Go Library Bag pattern (pullout page P1).

Main print

- 1 rectangle 8˝ × 28˝ for the side lining
- 1 rectangle 7˝ × 11˝ for the bottom lining
- 2 rectangles 7¼˝ × 8˝ for the exterior
- 1 binding strip 2˝ × width of fabric

White print

- 2 rectangles 7¼˝ × 8˝ for the pocket back
- 2 rectangles 7¼˝ × 2½˝ for the zippered pocket

Accent print: 4 rectangles 7¼˝ × 5½˝ for the pocket

Bottom print: 1 rectangle 7˝ × 11˝ for the bottom exterior

Fusible interfacing

- 4 rectangles 7¼˝ × 8˝ for the exterior and pocket backs
- 2 rectangles 7¼˝ × 5½˝ for the pocket
- 1 rectangle 7¼˝ × 2½˝ for the zippered pocket
- 1 bottom

20˝-wide fusible webbing

- 1 rectangle 8˝ × 28˝
- 1 rectangle 7˝ × 11˝

20˝-wide foam stabilizer

- 1 rectangle 8˝ × 28˝
- 1 rectangle 8˝ × 12˝

Instructions

Seam allowances are ¼˝ unless otherwise noted.

PREPARE THE EXTERIOR FABRIC

Following the manufacturer's instructions, press to adhere the fusible interfacing to the wrong side of the pocket backs, 2 accent pockets, the zippered pocket, and the bottom. Trim the bottom along the edge of the interfacing.

MAKE THE ZIPPERED POCKET

1. Lay the zipper on an interfaced 7¼˝ × 5½˝ pocket piece with right sides together and the zipper aligned with a long edge of the pocket. You will be able to see the wrong side of the zipper. Pin the zipper in place. Stitch together using a zipper foot, sewing close to the zipper-tape edge. Backstitch to secure. ┆ A

2. Lay an un-interfaced 7¼˝ × 5½˝ pocket on top of the zipper, matching the top and side edges of the bag exterior with right sides together. Pin in place. Sew through all layers using a zipper foot. ┆ B

3. Reposition the fabrics wrong sides together and press. Topstitch ⅛˝ from the folded edge. ┆ C

4. In the same manner, sew the 2 white-print pocket rectangles to the other side of the zipper tape. It should measure 7¼˝ × 8˝. ┆ D

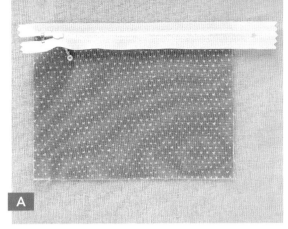

A

B

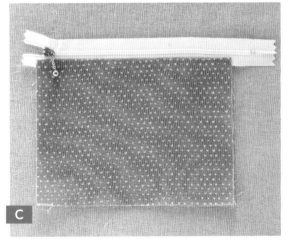

C

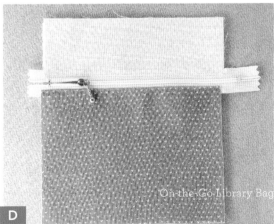

D

MAKE THE OPEN POCKET AND ADD THE POCKET BACKS

1. Pin together the zipper pocket and a 7¼″ × 8″ pocket back. Trim the excess zipper if you started with a longer zipper (like I did). Set aside.

2. Right sides together, sew the 2 remaining 7¼″ × 5½″ pockets along a long edge. Reposition the fabrics with the wrong sides together and press.

3. Pin the open pocket to a 7¼″ × 8″ pocket back, matching the bottom edges. Set aside. ┆ E

ASSEMBLE THE BAG

1. Sew the open pocket unit to a main-print side rectangle along one side. Sew the zippered pocket unit to the other main-print side rectangle along one side. ┆ F

2. Sew the pairs together to make the bag tube. ┆ G

3. At the bottom edge of the bag tube, mark the center of each pocket and the center of each side. Also mark the center points of the exterior bottom. Match up the centers first and pin the bottom to the sides. ┆ H

E

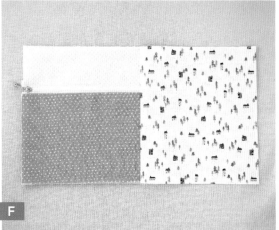

F

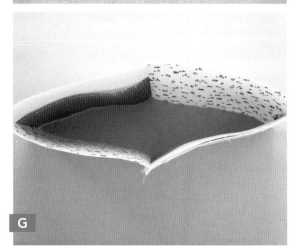

G

H

4. Remove the extension table of your sewing machine. This will help you rotate the bag around the machine as you sew. Lay the bag on your sewing machine with the bag side on top and the bag bottom on the bottom. Start sewing along a straight side and slow down when you sew the curved side. One stitch at a time and with the needle down, stitch around each curve. ┊ I & J

tip

Clip all 4 curved seam allowances for the smooth round sides. Make sure the seam allowances are exactly ¼˝. Sew again if the seams are narrow or bigger than ¼˝. This helps ensure an even, round shape.

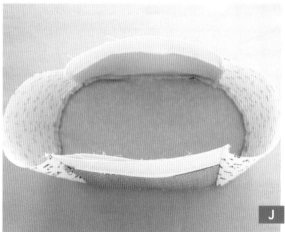

Make the Lining

1. Center and fuse the bottom lining rectangle onto the 8˝ × 12˝ foam stabilizer using fusible webbing. If you don't have fusible webbing, pin the lining to the foam stabilizer and quilt them together. Trace the bottom pattern (pullout page P1) onto the assembled fabric and trim the excess.

tip

If you use different batting (like medium-weight fusible batting or cotton batting), check the fit before trimming. The thickness of the batting may cause the size to be slightly different.

2. Center and fuse the side lining rectangle onto the 8˝ × 28˝ foam stabilizer using fusible webbing. Trim to 26¾˝ × 7½˝.

3. Sew the side lining together along the short edges to make a tube. Stitch the tube to the bottom lining, following Assemble the Bag, Steps 2–4 (pages 56 and 57), except use a ⅜˝ seam allowance for a tight fit to the exterior. ┊ K

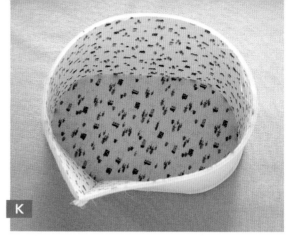

4. Trim the batting from the seam allowances to give a nice finished shape.

5. Put the lining inside the bag and pin in place. Fold the binding strip in half lengthwise, wrong sides together, and press. Re-pin to attach the binding strip to the top of the bag/lining assembly, matching the raw edges of the bag. Sew all the way around. ┊ L

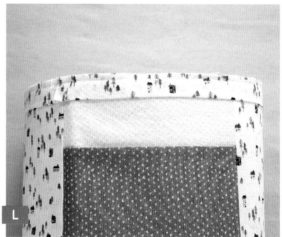

6. Fold the binding to the inside and hand stitch it to the bag lining.

Add the Handles
Mark the handle placement 1˝ inside the pocket and side seams. Using matching or contrasting heavyweight thread, backstitch the leather handles in place on each outer panel to finish, making sure that they sit opposite of each other. ┊ M & N

tip

Optional: If you don't have a leather handle set, you can use leather strips and attach them using rivets.

MODERN STRING BAG

Finished bag: 8″ wide × 8¾″ high × 7″ deep

This project was inspired by my friend's lunch bag, a traditional drawstring bag featuring a busy print. I wanted to make a more modern version, so I added a zipper pocket on one side and an open pocket on the other. I highly recommend using Décor-Bond for structure. And if you want to use this pattern for a lunch bag, just change the cotton batting to insulated batting. I hope you enjoy this one-of-a-kind bag!

Materials and Supplies

Dimensions are written width × height throughout.

Linen: Fat quarter for bag body

Print 1: Fat quarter for open pocket

Print 2: Fat quarter for zipper pocket

Print 3: ½ yard for gusset

Lining: ⅔ yard

Binding: ⅛ yard

Fusible interfacing: ½ yard (I used Pellon 809 Décor-Bond; I got mine from dailylike.ca. You can also use 1 yard of Pellon 520 Deco-Fuse.)

Batting: ½ yard

¼″-diameter cotton cord: 1½ yards

1″-wide cotton ribbon: 1½″ length

½″-diameter grommets: 4 sets

8″ lace zipper

Cutting

The bag body and gusset top will be cut during the instructions (page 63). See the Modern String Bag patterns (pullout page P1).

Linen: 2 rectangles 8½″ × 9″ for the bag body

Print 1: 1 rectangle 8½″ × 9½″ for the open pocket

Print 2: 1 rectangle 8½″ × 9½″ for the zipper pocket

Print 3: 1 rectangle 7½″ × 25″ for the gusset

Lining

• 2 rectangles 9½″ × 10″

• 1 rectangle 8½″ × 25″

Binding: 1 strip 1¼″ × width of fabric for the single binding

Fusible interfacing

• 2 rectangles 8½″ × 9″ for the bag body

• 2 rectangles 8½″ × 4¾″ for the pockets

• 1 rectangle 7½″ × 25″ for the gusset

Batting

• 2 rectangles 10″ × 10½″ for the bag body

• 1 rectangle 10″ × 27″ for the gusset

Instructions

Seam allowances are ¼˝ unless otherwise noted.

PREPARE THE EXTERIOR PIECES

Fuse the interfacing to the wrong side of the bag body pieces and the gusset. Fuse the pocket interfacings to the pockets, aligning the bottom long edges. Press the pockets in half and set aside.

MAKE THE ZIPPERED POCKET

1. Use masking tape to attach the lace zipper on top of the zipper pocket, aligning the top of the zipper pocket right under the zipper teeth. Topstitch in place. ┆ **A**

2. Pin the zipper pocket to the linen bag body, aligning the bottom edges. Trace the round corner using the body pattern. Stitch around the sides and bottom of the unit with an ⅛˝ seam to attach the pocket to the linen rectangle. Trim the excess. Mark the bottom center. ┆ **B**

3. Topstitch the other side of the lace zipper to the linen.

MAKE THE OPEN POCKET

Pin the open pocket to the front of the other linen bag body, aligning the bottom edges. Trace the round corners, stitch, and trim the excess as in Make the Zippered Pocket, Step 2 (at left). Mark the bottom center and set aside.

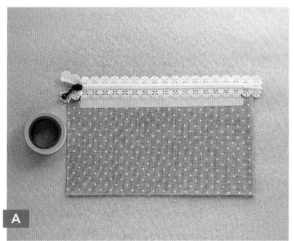

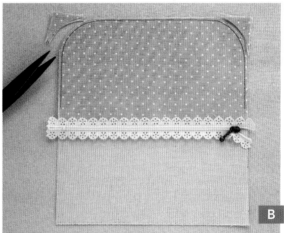

ASSEMBLE THE BAG

1. Trace both ends of the gusset using the gusset top pattern. Mark the center of the gusset lengthwise; it should be 12½″ from the end. Matching up the marked centers, pin the gusset to the zipper pocket unit. ┆ C

2. Remove the extension table of your sewing machine. This will help you rotate the bag around the machine as you sew.

Lay the bag on your sewing machine with the gusset on top and the pocket unit on the bottom. Start sewing from the bag opening and slow down when you sew the round side. Clip the round corner seam for easy sewing. One stitch at a time and with the needle down, rotate your bag clockwise. ┆ D

3. In the same manner, pin the open pocket side to other side of the gusset and finish sewing the bag exterior. ┆ E

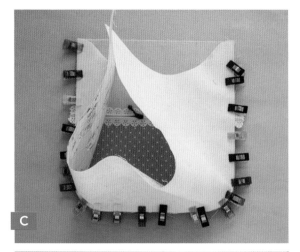

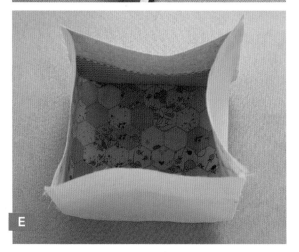

Add the Lining

1. Center and baste the lining pieces to the batting. Quilt as desired (I sewed straight lines 1″ apart). Trim the side gusset to 7½″ × 25″. Trace the gusset top and 2 body linings using the patterns.

2. Join the gusset and body in the same manner as Assemble the Bag, Step 2 (previous page), but use a ⅜″ seam allowance for a tight fit to the exterior. ⋮ **F & G**

Assemble the Binding

1. Put the lining inside the bag, wrong sides together, and pin in place. Trim the lining if necessary. ⋮ **H**

2. Align a single binding strip to the exterior, right sides together and matching the raw edges at the top of the bag. Re-pin. Fold the end of the binding in about ½″ and sew the binding to the bag exterior. Sew over about ½″ of the beginning binding end and trim the excess. Fold in the seam allowance to the inside and hand stitch to finish the binding. ⋮ **I**

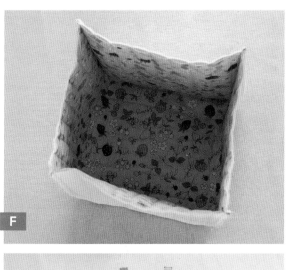

F

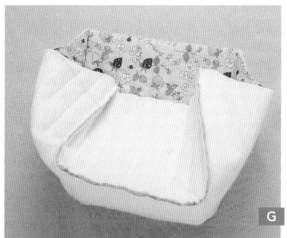

G

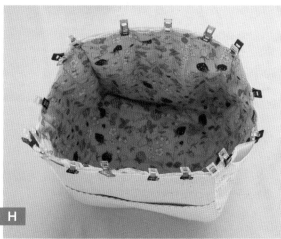

H

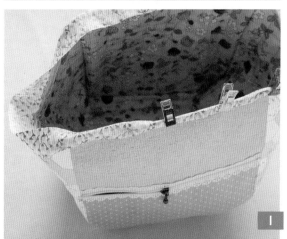

I

FINISH THE BAG

1. Fold the bag sides in half. Hand stitch right under the binding end to help with easy folding. ┊ J

2. Mark the grommet holes using the bag pattern. Attach the grommets following the manufacturer's instructions.

3. Tape the end of the cotton cord with some packing tape and thread it through the grommets as shown. Adjust the length as needed (I used about 50″ of cord). Tape the ends of the cords together.

4. Wrap the taped cord ends together with cotton ribbon and sew to secure, making sure to stitch through the ribbon and the cord. ┊ K

tips

- For easy closing and opening, I used the tape method instead of tying a knot.

- If you have one, use a ½″ punch for the grommet hole. If not, clip the outer fabric using a pair of scissors and cut out each layer separately.

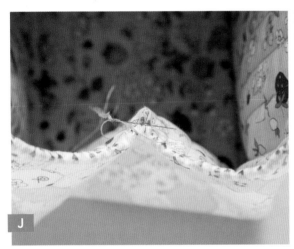

SMALL DOME PURSE

Finished purse without handles: 10˝ wide × 6½˝ high × 5˝ deep

I like to make oddly shaped bags in triangular, oval, or dome shapes, as I did with this purse. When I designed this bag, I was so happy with its simple structure yet unique shape. For easy opening and closing, I recommend using a double-slide zipper. Try low-volume fabric or contrasting prints. Depending on your fabric choice, this purse is suitable for all ages!

Materials and Supplies

Dimensions are written width × height throughout.

Print 1: Fat quarter *or* ⅓ yard for purse exterior (If your fabric is directional, you may need more fabric to cut the rectangle lengthwise.)

Print 2: Fat eighth *or* ¼ yard

Lining: ½ yard

Binding: ⅛ yard

Foam stabilizer: 1 yard (I prefer ByAnnie's Soft and Stable or Pellon FF77 Flex-Foam.)

Heavyweight thread, such as hand-quilting thread, for handle attachment

Leather handle: 1 set 15½˝ (I got mine from byhandsusa.com.)

15˝ double-slide zipper

Cutting

Print 1: 1 rectangle 11˝ × 18˝ for the purse exterior

Print 2: 1 rectangle 20˝ × 5½˝ for the zipper gusset

Lining

• 1 rectangle 13˝ × 20˝ for the body lining

• 1 rectangle 22˝ × 7½˝ for the zipper-gusset lining

Binding: 1 strip 1½˝ × width of fabric for the single-fold binding (If you prefer double-fold binding, cut the strip 2˝ × width of fabric.)

Foam stabilizer

• 1 rectangle 12˝ × 19˝ for the body

• 1 rectangle 21˝ × 6½˝ for the zipper gusset

Instructions

Seam allowances are ¼″ unless otherwise noted.

For the purse body and zipper gusset, see the Small Dome Purse patterns (pullout page P1).

MAKE THE BAG BODY

Layer the purse exterior and lining rectangles wrong sides together, with the foam stabilizer in the middle. Baste and quilt as desired (I quilted crisscross lines approximately ¾″ apart). Trace the body pattern and trim the excess. Mark the center on both sides, referring to the pattern. | A

MAKE THE ZIPPER GUSSET

1. Center the zipper gusset on top of the foam stabilizer, right side up. Place the zipper-gusset lining on top of the gusset, right side down. Pin the layers together. Referring to the pattern, mark a ½″ × 15″ rectangle in the center for the zipper opening. Mark the centerline and the small triangles at each end of the rectangle. Sew on the marked rectangle. For the cleanest finish, start about halfway down a long side, stitch around the rectangle, and then overlap where you started sewing by about ½″. | B

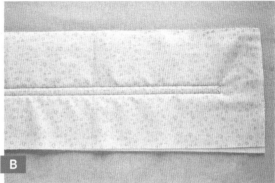

2. Cut along the centerline, just to the tip of the marked triangle. Then clip as far as you can into the corners along the marked lines, making sure not to clip the stitching. | C

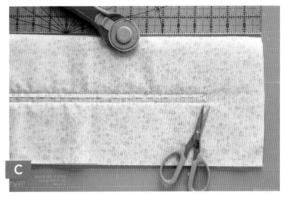

3. Trim the foam stabilizer away from the seam allowances to reduce bulk. | D

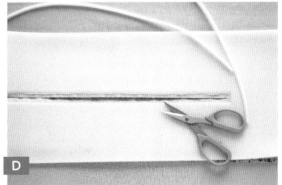

4. Pull the lining through the opening to the wrong side of the zipper gusset. Press. | E

Add the Zipper

1. Place the zipper under the opening and make sure the zipper teeth are aligned lengthwise at the center. Secure the zipper using double-sided fabric tape or masking tape. Topstitch ⅛″ from the edge around the opening through all layers. As you approach the zipper pull, stop and unzip the zipper about halfway to get the zipper pull out of the way. Continue stitching. ┆ F

2. Quilt straight lines approximately ½″ apart using matching thread. Mark the center of the zipper length. Trace the zipper gusset pattern, matching the center mark. Trim the excess. Mark the center on both sides, referring to the pattern. ┆ G

ASSEMBLE THE BAG

1. Matching up the center marks, place the bag body and zipper gusset right sides together. Clip or pin. ┆ H

2. Remove the extension table of your sewing machine. This will help you rotate the bag around the machine as you sew. Lay the bag on your sewing machine with the zipper gusset on top and the bag body on the bottom. Start sewing on a straight side first and slow down when you sew the round side. One stitch at a time and with the needle down, rotate your purse counterclockwise.

tip

Clip the round seam allowances for smooth, round sides. Make sure your seam allowances are ¼″ even. Sew again if the seams are too narrow or are bigger than ¼″. This helps ensure an even, round shape.

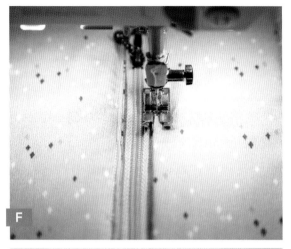

F

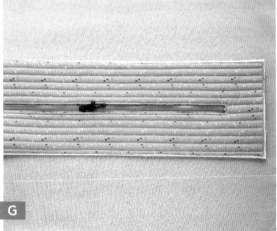

G

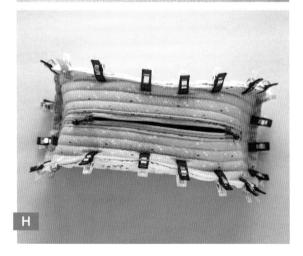

H

3. With right sides together, align a single binding strip to the raw edges of the gusset and re-pin. Fold the beginning of the binding in about ½″ and sew the binding to the gusset. Sew over the ½″ at the beginning and trim the excess. ┆ I & J

4. Turn the binding edge ¼″ to the inside; then finger-press the folded edge over to the inside of the bag. Hand stitch it in place. ┆ K

ADD THE HANDLES

Mark the handle placement from the bag body pattern, making sure that the handles will sit opposite each other. Using matching or contrasting heavyweight thread, hand stitch the leather handles in place on each outer panel to finish (I used a backstitch). ┆ L

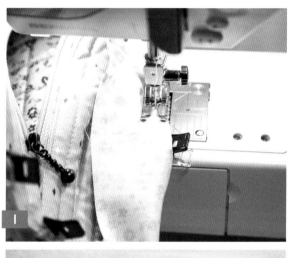

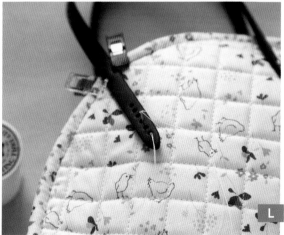

STRAWBERRY WOOL CASE

Finished case: 7″ × 9½″

The combination of wool felt and hand embroidery creates delicate details and unique texture. By repeating simple motifs with no fancy appliqué, anybody can design their own patterns. You can also twist this project by stitching only one strawberry for a pincushion or by changing the number of motifs.

Materials and Supplies

Dimensions are written width × height throughout.

Assorted wool felt scraps for appliqué pieces

Yarn-dyed cotton: ¼ yard for front cover and binding

Print 1: Fat quarter *or* scrap at least 7″ × 10″ for case back

Print 2: 2″ × 9½″ scrap for case side

Lining: Fat quarter

Clear vinyl: ¼ yard (I like Premium Clear Vinyl by C&T Publishing or by ByAnnie.)

Woven fusible interfacing: ¼ yard (I used Pellon SF101 Shape-Flex.)

Fusible fleece: ⅓ yard

Fusible tape, such as Steam-A-Seam 2 double-stick fusible tape

Embroidery floss to match felt colors

9″ zippers: 2

Elastic band: 3½″ × ½″ *(optional)*

Cotton label: 1½″ × 2½″ *(optional)*

Cutting

For the strawberry motifs, see the Strawberry Wool Case patterns (pullout page P1).

Yarn-dyed cotton

- 1 rectangle 6½″ × 9½″
- 1 binding strip 2½″ × width of fabric

Print 1: 1 rectangle 6½″ × 9½″

Lining

- 1 rectangle 14″ × 9½″
- 1 strip 2″ × 9½″
- 2 strips 1½″ × 9½″ for the zipper binding

Clear vinyl: 2 rectangles 5¾″ × 9½″

Woven fusible interfacing: 1 rectangle 6½″ × 9½″

Fusible fleece: 1 rectangle 14″ × 9½″

Strawberry Wool Case   75

Instructions

Seam allowances are ¼″ unless otherwise noted.

See Embroidery Stitches (page 111) for instructions on how to make the stitches.
Use 3 strands of embroidery floss for all hand embroidery.

APPLIQUÉ AND STITCH THE DESIGN

1. Trace the strawberry patterns to assorted felt scraps using a fabric marker. Cut out all the felt pieces. In the center of the 6½″ × 9½″ yarn-dyed cotton rectangle, draw a 5″ × 8″ guide box. Arrange each element in the guide box, referring to the placement pattern (pullout page P1). A

A

> *tip*
>
> **When you arrange the strawberries, leave room to hand stitch the stems and leaves later.**

2. Using pins or fusible tape, secure the felt elements for hand stitching. ┊ B

3. Whipstitch all the berries using 3 strands of embroidery floss. Chainstitch the stem and use a French knot stitch for the small berry seeds. Use the satin stitch for the berry leaves and 3 straight stitches for the big strawberry seeds. ┊ C

B

C

MAKE THE CASE EXTERIOR

1. *Optional:* Fold in the raw edges of the cotton label and sew it to the center of the case back, ⅛˝ from the folded edges.

2. Fuse woven fusible interfacing on the wrong side of the case back. Sew the appliqué front to the case side along the long edges. Then sew the case back to the other side of the case side, as shown. Press the seam allowances toward the center. The case exterior should measure 14˝ × 9½˝.

3. Press fusible fleece to the wrong side of the case exterior. | **D**

MAKE THE VINYL POCKETS

1. Fold the zipper binding strips in half lengthwise, wrong sides together, and press. Unfold. Bring the long raw edges toward the center crease on the wrong side. Press. Fold in half again and press. Wrap a long edge of a vinyl pocket piece with a binding strip and stitch ¹⁄₁₆˝ from the outer edge. Make 2. | **E**

tip

Place a scrap of fabric or paper under the vinyl to keep it from sticking to the sewing machine.

tip

If you'd like a little label on the back of your case, as shown on mine, add it to the case back before you fuse the woven fusible interfacing to the wrong side of the back. For this patch, I used a printed cotton ribbon.

D

E

2. Change to the zipper foot on your sewing machine. Sew a vinyl/binding piece to one zipper. Place the top edge of the binding ¼″ from the zipper teeth. Draw the ¼″ line on the zipper, if needed. ┆ F

3. Press both long edges of a 2″ × 9½″ lining strip ¼″ to the inside. Topstitch the strip to the other side of the zipper. ┆ G

4. Repeat Steps 2 and 3 to sew the other pocket and zipper to the other side of the lining strip. Make sure that both zipper pulls are at the same end when the zippers are closed. ┆ H

ASSEMBLE THE CASE

1. Place the case exterior wrong side up. Place the lining right side up on top of the case exterior.

2. Place the vinyl right side up on top of the lining and exterior. The zipper pulls should be at the top edge when the zippers are closed. Using binding clips, hold together all the layers in place.

3. *Optional:* Fold under both ends of the elastic and place it at the center of the pocket unit. ┆ I

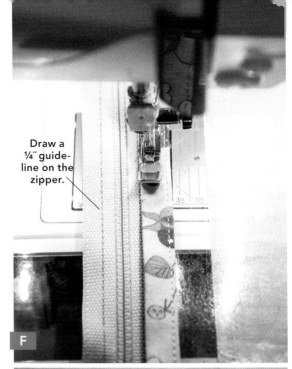

Draw a ¼″ guide-line on the zipper.

F

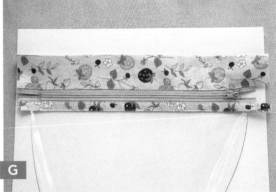

G

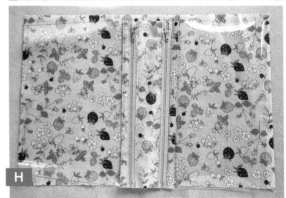

H

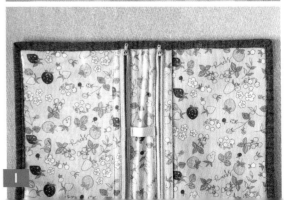

I

4. From the front of the case, stitch-in-the-ditch along each center seamline, matching your threads to both the top and bottom fabrics. This will define the sides of the case and secure the elastic to the inside. | J & K

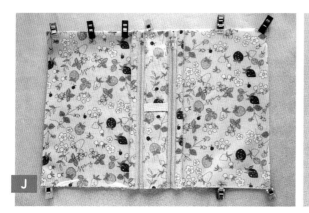

ATTACH THE BINDING

1. Fold the binding strip in half lengthwise, wrong sides together, and press. Sew the cover binding to the front side of the case. | L

tips

- Make sure not to sew the metal ends of the zipper when you sew the binding.

- If you prefer to use a blind stitch to finish the binding, sew the binding to the *lining side* of the case and finish the binding on the front.

2. Fold the edge of the binding strip to the inside of the case. Glue baste or use fusible tape to secure the binding. Place the appliquéd cover on your sewing machine. Align the edge of the binding with the middle of the walking foot, and adjust the needle position so that it is 1 mm from the edge of the lining side of the binding. Machine sew along the inside folded edge of the binding. Sew slowly when you approach the corners, and keep the needle down as you turn the corners. ┆ M & N

tip

Switch to a 100/16 or denim machine needle for this step if you have one. The heavier needles help when stitching bulky layers.

TRAVEL ORGANIZER

Finished organizer: 11½˝ wide × 8¼˝ high × 4˝ deep

It's good to have a clear view of all your supplies in a big pouch so that you don't have to go digging through everything. Two mesh pockets are perfect for organizing tools and notions, and you can enlarge or reduce the size for your purpose. If you use waterproof fabric and skip the batting, this organizer can be a good beach bag as well!

Materials and Supplies

Dimensions are written width × height throughout.

Exterior: ½ yard
(⅔ yard if directional)

Mesh fabric: 12˝ × 13˝ (I used ByAnnie's lightweight mesh fabric.)

Lining: ½ yard

Binding: ⅛ yard

Woven fusible interfacing:
11½˝ × 21˝ (I used Pellon SF101 Shape-Flex.)

Medium-weight fusible batting:
11½˝ × 21˝

Zippers: 1 double-slide 25˝ long (I got mine from byannie.com) and 2 regular, each 8˝ long

Cutting

For the bag body, see the Travel Organizer pattern (pullout page P2).

Exterior: 1 bag body (If the fabric is directional, like mine, cut 2 rectangles 10˝ × 12˝ and sew them together facing in opposite directions so they both will face upright when the bag is assembled.)

Mesh fabric: 2 rectangles 12˝ × 6½˝

Lining

• 1 bag body

• 4 rectangles 2˝ × 12˝ for the pocket binding (A)

• 4 rectangles 1½˝ × 12˝ for the zipper binding (B)

• 4 rectangles 1¼˝ × 3˝ for the pocket zipper tabs (C)

• 2 rectangles 1½˝ × 5˝ for the bag closing strips (D)

Binding: 2 strips 2½˝ × 26˝

Woven fusible interfacing: 1 bag body

Medium-weight fusible batting: 1 bag body

Instructions

Seam allowances are ¼˝ unless otherwise noted.

PREPARE THE EXTERIOR FABRIC

Fuse the fusible interfacing to the wrong side of the exterior fabric. Fuse the fusible batting on top of the fusible interfacing for a double layer of interfacing. ⦙ A

MAKE THE ZIPPER POCKET

1. Fold the zipper tab (C) ends ¼˝ toward the inside and press. Fold in half and press again. Slide a zipper end into each one and top-stitch along the folded edge. ⦙ B

2. Center the zipper on a 2˝ × 12˝ pocket binding strip (A), right sides together. You will be able to see the wrong side of the zipper. Pin the zipper in place. Stitch together using a zipper foot, sewing close to the zipper tape edge. Backstitch to secure.

3. With right sides together, lay a 2˝ × 12˝ pocket binding strip (A) on the zipper, matching the top edges. Pin in place. Sew through all layers using a zipper foot. ⦙ C

4. Reposition the fabrics with wrong sides together. Press. ⦙ D

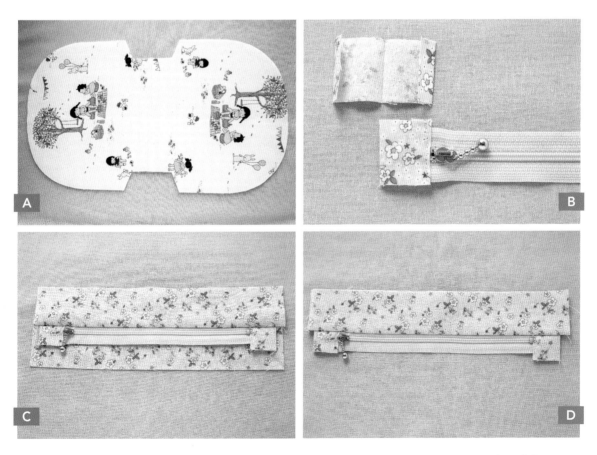

5. Fold 2 zipper binding strips (B) 1½″ × 12″ in half lengthwise, wrong sides together. Press. Unfold and bring the long raw edges toward the center crease on the wrong side of the fabric. Press. Fold in half lengthwise again and press. Slide the mesh rectangle into a binding strip, and hold it in place with binding clips. Sew the binding to the mesh fabric, ⅛″ from the inner folded edge. ¦ E

6. Place the mesh pocket on the zipper, positioning the zipper tape under the binding. Sew the binding to the other side of the zipper from Step 4. ¦ F

7. Place the pocket on top of the lining, right sides up, and pin in place. Place the second binding strip on the bottom edge of the mesh rectangle. Topstitch just inside both edges. ¦ G

8. Repeat Steps 2–7 to make a second pocket and attach it to the other side of the body. The zipper pulls should be at the top edge when the zippers are closed. Place the pocket unit wrong side up, and place the lining wrong side up on top of the pocket unit. Sew ⅛″ inside all the way around the edge. Trim the excess. ¦ H

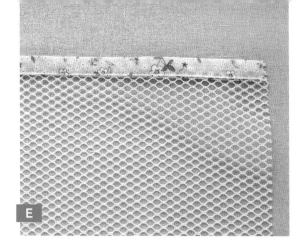

E

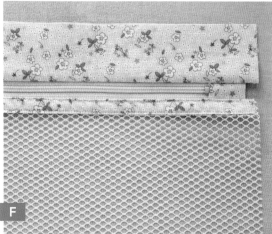

F

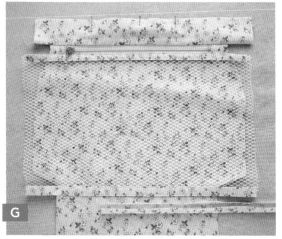

G

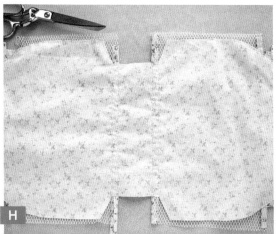

H

ASSEMBLE THE BAG

1. Place the bag exterior wrong side up. Place the pocket/lining unit right side up on top of the bag exterior. Using binding clips, hold all the layers in place. | I

2. Fold the binding strip in half length-wise, wrong sides together, and press. Pin the binding strip to the exterior, aligning the raw edges. Sew to the exterior with a ⅜″ seam. | J

3. Press the folded edge of the binding toward the lining; glue baste. Machine stitch just to the right of the binding seam. | K

4. Align a double-slide zipper with the exterior top edge, aligning the zipper teeth right under the binding edge. Pin in place and machine stitch right under the binding edge, as shown. | L & M

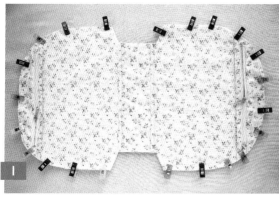

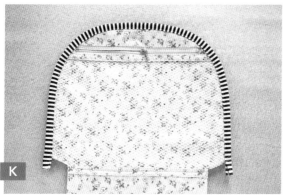

5. Open the zipper and repeat Step 4 for the other side of the zipper.

6. Turn the pouch inside out. On each side, fold at the inside corners and match the raw edges, aligning the seam at the end of the zipper with the center of the pouch bottom. Place the bag closing strip (D) wrong side up. Fold both short ends of the strip toward the wrong side and pin. Stitch across the raw edges. Backstitch at the beginning and end of the seam to secure. ┊ N

7. Fold in the remaining raw edge of the strip, as shown, and topstitch. Repeat for the other side of the organizer. ┊ O

PATCHWORK BASKET

Finished basket: 10½″ wide × 5¼″ high × 3½″ deep

In this basket pattern, I show you how to assemble a three-dimensional basket from a flat piece of patchwork. The basket takes shape as you sew the outer patchwork squares together—no extra seams! The secret is knowing which squares to sew together first. Once you figure out the assembly, you can adopt the technique for other projects, like making a basket with a zipper closure or changing the block size for a smaller case.

Materials and Supplies

Dimensions are written width × height throughout.

Assorted print scraps: You will need 34 squares 3″ × 3″ for the patchwork. (I cut 3 squares *each* from 13 prints.)

Lining: ½ yard

Binding: ⅛ yard

Foam stabilizer: 16″ × 15″ (ByAnnie's Soft and Stable or Pellon FF77 Flex-Foam works well.)

Cotton batting: ⅔ yard

Optional handle supplies:

Print: 16″ × 5″

Poly strap: 14″ × 1½″ (I used ByAnnie's Polypro Strapping.)

Double-cap rivets: 2 sets

Cutting

Lining: 1 square 15″ × 15″

Binding: 1 strip 2½″ × width of fabric

Cotton batting: 1 square 22″ × 22″

Instructions

Seam allowances are ¼″ unless otherwise noted.

ASSEMBLE THE SQUARES

1. Sew together 2 print squares for the first row, which will be the top left corner of the patchwork center. Sew the blocks together in diagonal rows, as shown in the finished patchwork base (below). Press the seam allowances of each row in alternating directions.

> ### tip
>
> When arranging the prints, do not use the same-color print on the outer side edges because they will be sewed together next.

2. Join the rows to make the basket exterior. Press the seams toward the outside from the center diagonal line.

3. Center the patchwork section on top of the batting and baste. Quilt as desired. ┊ A

4. Trim the top and bottom, leaving a ¼″ seam beyond the square corners, as shown. ┊ B

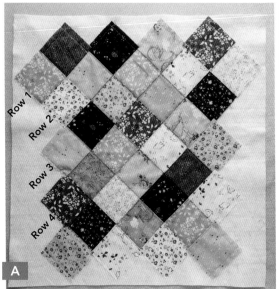

A

Finished patchwork base

B

MAKE THE BASKET EXTERIOR

1. Remove a couple of end stitches and clip ¼˝ of the center block seam, as shown. ┊ **C & D**

2. With right sides together, join the first 2 blocks. ┊ **E**

3. In the same manner, clip the next ¼˝ seam as shown. ┊ **F**

4. With right sides together, sew the sets of 2 squares that are next to each other together, stopping ¼˝ from the end of the seam. Make sure the corners are matching. ┊ **G**

5. Clip a ¼˝ square from the end of the seam allowance. ┊ H

6. Sew the remaining squares together to finish the basket shape. ┊ I–K

7. Repeat Steps 1–6 for the other side of the basket to finish the exterior. ┊ L

MAKE THE LINING

1. Center the lining, right side up, on top of the foam stabilizer and quilt as desired (I quilted crisscross lines 1″ apart). Trim to 15″ × 14″.

2. Fold in half lengthwise and sew both ends to make an envelope shape. This unit should measure 14¼″ × 7″.

3. Fold each corner flat, with the seam centered. Mark and stitch a line 3½″ long across the point. Trim the excess. ┊ M & N

ASSEMBLE THE BASKET

1. Put the lining inside the basket, wrong sides together. Clip in place. ┊ O

2. Fold the binding strip in half lengthwise, wrong sides together, and press. Re-pin to secure the binding to the outer edge of the basket, matching the raw edges. Sew the binding, exterior, and lining together along the top edge. ┊ P

3. Near the binding ends, leave about 5˝ unsewn and mark where the binding should meet. Sew the ends together, being sure to backstitch to lock the stitch. Trim the excess and sew the binding to the basket. Fold the binding to the inside of the basket. Hand stitch to finish. ┊ Q

Add the Handle (Optional)

1. Fold in 1˝ along all edges of the 16˝ × 5˝ print fabric and press as shown. Wrap the poly strap with the print fabric and press as shown. ┊ R

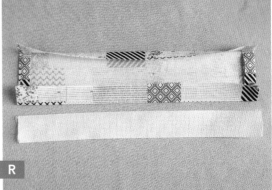

2. Topstitch all the way around the outer edge and down the length of the center to finish the handle. ┊ S

3. Mark the center of the basket and attach the handle using double-cap rivets, following the manufacturer's instructions. Or you can machine sew the handle to the basket.

Press both sides to help form the shape.

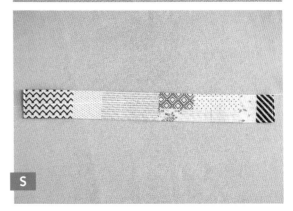

Leave the handle off for an open basket, or add a zippered top to hold everything inside.

SEWING STUDIO WALLHANGING

Finished wallhanging: 27½″ × 27½″

Ever since I started sewing, my favorite motif is a sewing machine! I drew it on a card for my sewing friend and I stitched it on a zipper pouch to store notions. Then I drew it on linen as a framed piece of wall art in my first book, *Sew Illustrated*. Now I want to hang it on my sewing room wall, as it's my sign. I hope it welcomes your guests and introduces yourself well.

Materials and Supplies

Dimensions are written width × height throughout.

Assorted print scraps: Enough for 65 squares 2″ × 2″ for patchwork

White print: 1 yard for background

Backing: 1 yard

Print scraps for spool and handwheel

Binding: ⅓ yard

Fusible web, like Lite Steam-a-Seam 2

Cotton batting: 1 yard

Thread: Dark brown and red (12-weight preferred) for stitched illustration and neutral (ivory) for quilting

Walking foot

Basting spray *or* curved safety pins

Masking tape

Cutting

Assorted print scraps: 65 squares 2″ × 2″

White print: 1 square 28″ × 28″

Backing: 1 square 30″ × 30″

Print scraps

• 1 square 3″ × 3″ for spool

• 2 rectangles 2″ × ½″ for spool

• 1 rectangle 2″ × 8″ for handwheel

Binding: 3 strips 2½″ × width of fabric

Cotton batting: 1 square 29″ × 29″

Sewing Studio Wallhanging

Instructions

Seam allowances are ¼˝ unless otherwise noted. For the sewing machine appliqué and wording, see the Sewing Studio Wallhanging pattern (pullout page P2).

MAKE THE PATCHWORK SEWING MACHINE

1. Sew together 3 print squares for the first segment of the first row, which will be the top left corner of the sewing machine. Continue to sew the blocks together in horizontal rows as shown, referring also to the finished quilt photo. Press the seam allowances in alternating directions from row to row. ┊ A

2. Join the rows to make the quilt center. Press the seam allowances as desired. I pressed each row to one side. Sew the 2˝ × 8˝ rectangle for the sewing machine handwheel onto the right end of the patchwork. ┊ B

3. Trace the sewing machine from the pattern onto paper or template plastic; cut it out on the line. Turn the traced template over and trace the *reversed* pattern onto the paper side of the fusible web. Fuse the web to the wrong side of the patchwork. Cut out the sewing machine on the line. ┊ C

APPLIQUÉ AND STITCH THE DESIGN

1. Draw a guideline 9˝ from the bottom of the background print and place the sewing machine centrally, matching the guideline. Press.

2. In the same manner, cut out the spool and fuse as shown. ┊ D

3. Make a copy of the wording (pullout page P2) and place it under the background fabric. Trace the wording using a temporary fabric pen. ┊ E

Photo by Kelly Burgoyne of C&T Publishing, Inc.

4. Make a quilt sandwich: Place the backing fabric right side down; then center the batting and then the quilt top right side up. The backing is slightly larger than the batting, which is larger than the quilt top layer. Baste them together using temporary basting spray or pins. Change to a walking foot, set to a 3.0 stitch length, and quilt as desired (I quilted straight vertical lines ½″ apart). **F**

F

G

tips

- Place the backing fabric on a large table or the floor and tape each side to prevent it from moving while you layer the quilt sandwich.

- When quilting straight lines, sew the first lines 1″ apart and then sew centerlines between the sewn lines.

5. Adjust the machine's stitch length to 3.0. Using dark 12-weight thread and a size 90 needle, top-stitch twice just inside the design.

tip

For the bobbin, match the thread color to the backing fabric, not the dark thread on top.

6. Change to red thread to stitch the word "sewing" and the length of thread. You won't need to change the bobbin thread color. Be sure to backstitch at the beginning and end.

7. Hand stitch the word "studio" using 2 strands of dark brown thread. **G**

FINISH THE QUILT

Trim to 27½″ × 27½″.

Attach the Binding

1. Join the 2½″ binding strips end to end with diagonal seams. Trim the seam allowances to ¼″ and press them open. Fold the binding strip in half lengthwise, wrong sides together, and press.

2. With raw edges together, stitch the binding to the edge of the wallhanging front, mitering the corners as you go.

3. Turn the binding over and stitch the folded edge to the back of the wallhanging. Machine stitch or hand stitch it in place.

tip

For machine-finished binding, attach the binding to the front in the usual way. Fold the binding to the back and glue baste it in place, making sure it covers the previous seamline by at least ⅛″. Turn the piece to the front and stitch just to the right of the binding seam through all the layers. It will catch the binding folded over to the back but from the front.

SCOOTER PILLOW

Finished pillow: 20″ × 20″

Someday, I wish to own a cute scooter and ride to my favorite bakery in the early morning. First, I designed my Someday fabric with a scooter motif, and here I made a set of scooter pillows. Dreams come true if they are alive in our minds! You can also make this design into a wallhanging or a table topper by forgoing the pillow back and just quilting and binding the pillow top.

Materials and Supplies

Dimensions are written width × height throughout.

Assorted prints: 9, plus 1 white solid for appliqué pieces

White print: ⅝ yard for pillow-front background

Lining: ⅝ yard

Backing: ⅔ yard

Binding: ⅓ yard

Fusible web, such as Lite Steam-a-Seam 2

Cotton batting: ⅝ yard

Thread: White and dark brown (12-weight preferred) for stitched illustration (You can use 50-weight thread if you don't have thicker thread, but 12-weight threads add texture and help the stitches stand out.)

Optional free-motion quilting supplies:

Darning foot

Silicone mat (I used Supreme Slider) and quilting gloves

Cutting

For the reversed appliqué patterns and the complete pattern layout, see the Scooter Pillow patterns (pullout page P2).

White print: 1 square 21″ × 21″

Lining: 1 square 23″ × 23″

Backing: 2 rectangles 20″ × 15½″

Binding: 3 strips 2½″ × width of fabric

Cotton batting: 1 square 22″ × 22″

Instructions

Seam allowances are ¼″ unless otherwise noted.

APPLIQUÉ AND STITCH THE DESIGN

1. Lay the fusible web, paper side up, over the reversed patterns for the appliqué shapes (pullout page P2). Use a pencil to trace each appliqué shape, leaving ½″ between tracings. Cut out each fusible-web shape roughly ¼″ outside the traced lines.

2. Following the manufacturer's instructions, press each fusible-web shape onto the wrong side of your chosen fabrics; let cool. Cut out the fabric shapes on the drawn lines. Peel off the paper backings.

3. Place the pattern under the white-print background fabric as a guide. Arrange the cut-out elements on the background fabric. Fuse in place. ┆ A

tip

If your fabric is difficult to see through, you can use transfer paper to transfer the pattern to the background fabric.

When I use a dark background fabric, I copy the pattern, cut out the design, and trace the cut-out pieces onto the background.

4. Trace the remaining designs with a temporary marking pen. ┆ B

A

B

5. Place the batting under the background fabric. Pin or baste. Set up the sewing machine with white 12-weight thread in the upper spool holder, a size 90/14 needle, and a 3.0 stitch length. Sewing through all layers, slowly stitch just inside the edges of the appliqué, backstitching at the beginning and end of each stitched portion. ┊ C

6. Change to dark brown thread and stitch just the outer edges of the appliqué and marked lines. ┊ D

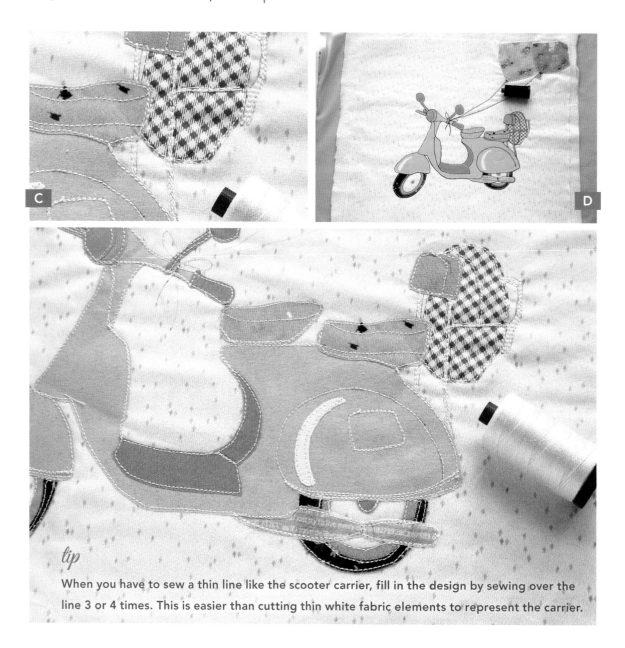

tip

When you have to sew a thin line like the scooter carrier, fill in the design by sewing over the line 3 or 4 times. This is easier than cutting thin white fabric elements to represent the carrier.

QUILT THE PILLOW TOP

1. Place the lining under the batting; pin or baste. Quilt as desired. For free-motion quilting, change to a darning foot, neutral 50-weight thread in the upper spool holder, and a size 80 needle. Drop the feed dogs and make one stitch. Pull the bobbin thread to the top and start with very short stitches to secure the quilting. Quilt the background around the scooter design to create an extra puffy texture. You can also quilt over the design if you wish. ┆ E–H

2. Trim off any excess batting and backing. Keeping the design centered, trim to 20″ × 20″.

MAKE THE PILLOW BACK

Fold one long edge of a backing fabric 20″ × 15½″ rectangle ½″ to the wrong side. Press. Fold over another 1½″ to the wrong side and press again. Topstitch along the edge of both folds and add straight lines ½″ apart to give extra strength. Repeat for the remaining pillow back. ┆ I

tip

If you are using a directional print, make sure the backing pieces are aligned in the right direction before sewing the pillow back.

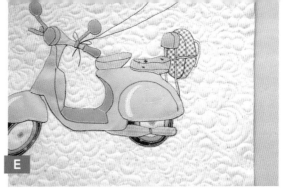
E

F

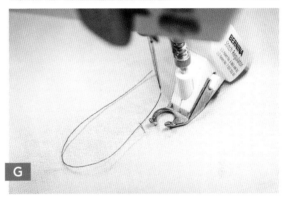
G

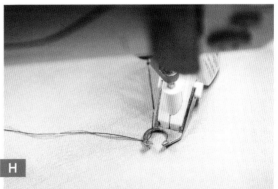
H

I

ASSEMBLE THE PILLOW

J

1. Place the quilted pillow front on a flat surface, right side down. Matching up the raw edges at the top of the pillow, place one backing rectangle faceup so the wrong sides of the back and front are together. The folded edge should run across the center of the pillow. Place the second backing rectangle with the raw edges aligned with the bottom of the pillow top. The folded backing edges will overlap at the center. Pin or sew ⅛″ from the edge to secure. ┊ J

2. Join the 2½″ binding strips end to end with a diagonal seam. Trim the seam allowance to ¼″ and press it open. Fold the binding strip in half lengthwise, wrong sides together, and press.

3. With the raw edges together, stitch the binding to the edge of the pillow front, mitering the corners as you go.

4. Turn the binding over; stitch the folded edge to the back of the pillow. Machine stitch or hand stitch it in place. ┊ K & L

K

L

tip

For machine-finished binding, attach the binding to the front in the usual way. Fold the binding to the back and glue baste it in place, making sure it covers the previous seamline by at least ⅛″. Turn the piece to the front and stitch just to the right of the binding seam through all the layers. It will catch the binding folded over to the back.

embroidery stitches

Chain Stitch

French Knot

Satin Stitch

Whipstitch

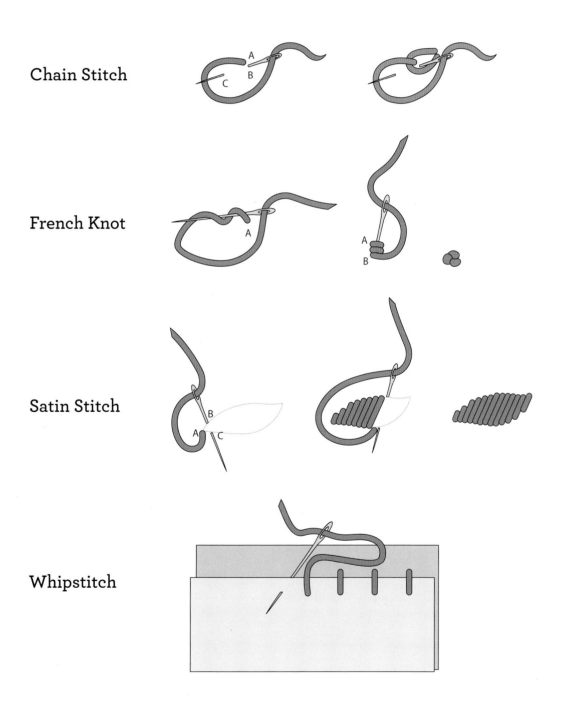

about the author

Minki Kim is a fabric and pattern designer with her own whimsical style. As a formally trained sculptor and self-taught sewist, she found that designing fabrics and creating art with fabric and thread were natural steps in her evolution as an artist.

Minki discovered sewing as a creative outlet when her children were small. She wanted to capture the beauty of ordinary moments, first with hand embroidery and later recreating them with her sewing machine and fabric—literally drawing with thread. Capturing ordinary moments in beautiful sewing illustrations to make keepsake snapshots of daily life has become her signature style.

Photo by Chloe Park

The author of *Sew Illustrated* and *Diary in Stitches* (both by C&T Publishing), Minki has also designed several fabric collections for Riley Blake Designs. She is originally from Korea but now calls Southern California home. She lives with her husband and three daughters.

Also by Minki Kim:

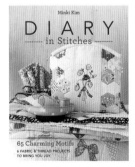

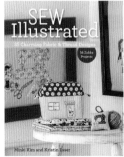

Visit Minki online and follow on social media!

Blog: minkikim.com

Pattern shop: sewingillustration.com

Pinterest: /zeriano

Instagram: @zeriano